CARNIVORES

In Praise of Carnivores

JANET DUBÉ

GOMER

First Impression—April 1997

ISBN 1 85902 413 0

This volume is published with the support of the Arts Council of Wales.

Printed in Wales at
Gomer Press, Llandysul, Ceredigion.

CONTENTS

	page
Children and blackberries	7
House, Gwyddgrug	9
over my head (i)	11
from *Meditations for our children* (one, two, three, four)	12
chickens and aeroplanes	15
Still life—(dawn chorus from the red armchair)	16
over my head (ii)	17
He came from Ceredigion	18
Lion and unicorn	20
Wedding	22
from *1982, a lament* (one, two, three, four)	23
as in the market (Carmarthen), 1982	28
After trying to read Susan Griffin	30
Diolch, Woody Guthrie	31
Advent poem for Jo	32
for Mrs Davies and Pencader Infants, Spring 1984	33
time for bed	34
midsummer sevens	35
Variations on Cherryblossom, Mayday 1984	36
in memoriam	37
View from the bus-stop: war memorial	38
changing forget-me-not	39
Sweet William and the Painted Lady	40
Viola Tricolour	41
Where the toadflax grows	42
Strip cartoon for radio	43
bird and iron, 1, 2, 3	45
The stormy winds that shift	48
October Frost, Llanllwni Mountain	50
Earthjuice	51
Praise be	57
In Praise of Carnivores	58

CONTENTS (*continued*)

Late snowdrops 60
May: i)Carmarthen 61
ii) Gwyddgrug 62
Collecting the milk 63
Nicotiana at New Road, Llandysul 64
heedless 65
The bonds of the world 66

Several of these poems first appeared in *New Welsh Review*.

Children and blackberries

Yesterday's world is
fading, like a tale told:
already here is dawn.

The haircut sheep, like
gentle schoolboys, eat
the grass by heart. A
boy pulls papers up
the hill on boards
between old pram wheels.
The empty schoolbus
waits outside the morning
shuttered pub. The youngest
children walk the hill
towards the oldest school, where
gravestones raise grey
birds and leaves above
the old stone wall. Here
ponies graze in someone's
garden, there in someone's
field. And someone's hands
have worked a rose
of coloured glass
to set above a door.
The busman, coalman
and the butcher say
good-day in English,
and it is. The paper
boy rides home on boards
with ropes between old wheels.
The watchdog next door
doesn't wake, and blackberries
are big and very sweet.

Yesterday's world is faded,
like a tale told. Children
and blackberries make
a good morning gentle.

House, Gwyddgrug

Jones Blaenblodau kept his eye
on the place, kept it locked,
kept the curtains drawn, kept
the rain out, kept his interest:

buzzards kept an eye too,
from higher, birds' eye view,
hovering, out of the blue:

sheep grazed to the back door
and the front: bleak sheep grazed
short the grass grown over stone,

but it was owls
who lived here, inhabited,
made this place home;

owls, on the dry stone ledge
in the old stone barn; owls
resting, leaving, returning;

owls, one by one, nesting,
rearing young, the young
resting, leaving, returning

maybe to rear their young;
and all the time, under the dry
stone ledge, for twelve years

grew the pile of owl pellets,
dry graves, among sticks
and straw, dry unblessed graves

of what the birds' eye view saw,
invisible to Jones, and sheep,
and me; mice, fledglings, moles

and voles; little grey brown
owl fodder; who lived here,
inhabited: made this place home.

over my head (i)

This room lost its ceiling
under snow
five seasons ago.

Now there are only slates
between me and birdsong,
me and the wet grey sky;

and looking up towards
the birdsong after rain
I see the wooden frame,

hundred year old beams
raised by Jac Llwyn's
auntie's dad.

The roof over my head,
the letter A:
beginnings

from Meditations for our Children

(one)

A wooden table,
four fresh field mushrooms:
the woodstove crackles.

The news from the sky
is: sunlight scatters
hasty rainbows
through the mountains.

The news from the hedgerows
is blue sloes and scarlet
rosehips, crabapples,
blackberries and nuts.

The news from the river
is renewal: springs leap
down the hills to fill
its swelling surge.
It moves, grey and huge
again, across the plain.

The news from my daughter
is clear and happy:
the news from my son
is that he carries a calculator
and is making a camera:

the news from my friends
is that babies will be born.

I have become ambitious for those babies.
I have become ambitious for their world.

(two)

I have done my poet's homework,
studied deaths and livings
in my secret poet's way:
what is there left to say?

rain on the roof
grey blue smoke scatters
the silver clock ticks raggedly

the radio on the table
the news on the radio

we are feathering our poisoned
nests with poisoned feathers

(three)

Beyond the yard, a plum tree
drifts and drops its yellow leaves
into the rain and scatty wind.

The near fields fall to the river,
the far fields rise to the hills,
green into grey, grey into blue
black, and the blue black
backs of the hills give in
to rich soft rain clouds.

Little one, take heart.
We are still lucky,
you and I. We eat daily.

(four)

I see dawn daily dress
the little living hills:

no black slag death pile
menaces my nights:

no chemists' fevered progress
explodes around my womb
or in the valley village;

no broken atoms are stored
restless nearby seeking death,

at least not yet. Nobody
wishes to kill or imprison
us for what we see as truth.

We eat daily. I see dawn
dress the living hills. Take
heart, we are insanely lucky.

chickens and aeroplanes

this writing, mystic picture
talk, Bright Star, daub
of Imagination's earthly
paw, would I were steadfast
as you are! Let flame,
immortal diamond's song, far
freedom's breath be sweet
upon my ear . . .

chickens and aeroplanes
and Jenkins' newlaid hedge:

Bowen's tractor hums and
meanders offstage left:

whose scenery is this?
whose audience? whose speech?

whose secret?

Still life—(dawn chorus from the red armchair)

The clock and the birds are friends,
they sing together: singing together
too, the clock and cat and cat and tap—

tick drip tock drop,
and the cat's trumpeted comfort,
the birds' speechless silver phrases.

We wanted silence and there is none.
The clock and the birds are friends,
and we: still life.

over my head (ii)

Crow, black rag, drops
behind the chimney pots,
and rises, riding the wind
over the blue slate roof;

building a nest
in my chimney,
stealing my fire.

He came from Ceredigion

He bargained in blood and breeding.
He invested in blood, his own,
his wife's, his rams'. He bred.

Through his blood came his land,
through his wife's came its life.
He invested his blood in his wife's

and it returned: four boys,
four girls. He invested his boys
in his land, he invested his girls

in its life: o silent joy, o fierce
solemnity, o hedges, water, grass
and grass, o stone, o wood,

o earth. His eyes were blue.
His children grew on stew,
potatoes, eggs. His wife—

o earth, o land, o mountain
hill and stream, o sacred
oak and ash. He built,

he bought, he sold, he won.
He drove his wife to vote,
he drove his rams to Builth,

he drove his bargains hard,
he drove his sons to win.
His wife; o distant sadness,

slippers, sweet remembrances,
o stove, o *cawl*, o bread
and jam. He watched the wrestling,

he built a silage pit.
His eyes were blue, he built
a bungalow. His hair was white.

His legs and arms were strong.
He drove his wife to church
(her feet were bad) o sad

o soft, o quiet talk, o rest.
He earned a bungalow. His wife—
(her feet were bad, her heart

was bad, the bags were packed)—
she died one night at home.
He lost, he moved; he died alone.

Lion and Unicorn

The lion and the unicorn
preside over the court
when justice is in session,
although their time is short,

because justice is expensive,
the court is closing down,
the lion and the unicorn
are moving out of town.

The lion and the unicorn
hanging on the wall,
presiding over justice,
looking rather small;

the lion and the unicorn
hanging on the crown:
did anybody catch them
moving out of town?

Justice didn't stay long.
Justice came and went.
The lion told the unicorn
the money's all been spent . . .

but how is it with you my dears
o how is it with you?
o did your children get the croup
and did you get the flu?

and are you sometimes late for work
and are they late for school?
and do you sometimes lose your rag
and are you sometimes cool?

and did you hope for better things,
and do you long for love?
o how is it with you my dears?
or do you long for love . . .

Pencader Courthouse, 1930 - 1990

Wedding

Blodeuwedd lives in a council house.
Her legs are nylon pantihose,
packets of three from the catalogue;
her crotch is chemically de-odourised,
her varicose veins have been stripped,
and her tubes are tied.

Blodeuwedd has human sons,
roots, flowers, appetites,
unemployment statistics,
big boots, ambition,
worn socks, a passion
for loud motorbikes and mating.

Blodeuwedd works part-time
in the cash and carry,
humps the shopping,
cooks the chips,
deals the dirt; and dances
at her sister's wedding.

from *1982, a lament*

(one)

When it's a fine day
and the house is quiet
and I'm on my own;

when the fire gets low
as the cat kills a bird
and the sun is blazing

on the daffodils; when
the chickens scratch
and cluck, scratch

and cluck, and the house
is quiet and the sun
is blazing on the rockery;

when the pale mauve
anemones are open to the sun
and the blue green daffodils

unsheath to yellow
in the blazing sun,
when the house is quiet

as the chickens scratch
and cluck and the lambs
learn to eat grass,

when the blue green
daffodils unsheath to yellow
as the jets scream overhead,

should I plant onions
or write a poem? Shall
I plant flowers or read

the paper? Would it
be better if I had a job
or is that part of the war

machine? is it better
to be certain
or uncertain? if I do

something for peace
does it help? if I do
something for peace

does it help peace
or does it help me?
if I do nothing
what does that mean?
Tell me, it's the one thing
I ever wanted to know, tell
me this one thing and I'll
never ask again, tell me
the truth, it's what I want
to know, I need to know,
tell me, how am I joined
to the war machine, tell me

can I get off?

(two)

I am teaching my heart to think
but she is a slow learner;
I wanted to write about daffodils
and already celandines are flowering
along the path; the sun

is blazing on the rockery.
On such a day we expect the jets
from Aberporth; the war machine
is so complex that the blue sky
is silent means war is nearer;

there are many disappeared in Argentina.
Every Thursday their women walk for them
around the square in Buenos Aires,
the handkerchiefs around their heads
engraved with names of disappeared.

She is speaking my language,
the woman who says 'that no more
lives may be lost, that no more
lives may be lost.' It is that
woman I understand, that woman
who speaks for me, that broken
english that is my tongue; cares,
you are my sister; *somos, venceremos*.

(three)

On the thirty-fifth day of the crisis,
just after nine-thirty in the morning,
(it was a sunny day)
I visited Carmarthen market.

On a stall near the sweets and ices,
across from the bootman's plastic awning
(Luther himself was away)
there were antiques and bric-a-brac;

you know the sort of thing I'm sure;
a set of scales in brass,
four wooden candlesticks, some glass,
and stuck at an angle, a union jack.

They don't make them like that anymore,
like I once waved on Empire Day.
This one was sold early in the morning.
I might have guessed there'd be a market

for an old union jack on a sunny day,
among the bric-a-brac at knockdown prices,
while half the population was still yawning
on the thirty-fifth day of the crisis.

(four)

Address to the arms traders and
the leaders of nations from
Maenclochog Village Hall,
June 4 1982

Gentlemen, this is the Mayor of Cardigan.

Her hair is white,
her figure slight:
her tongue is a dove,
plain as a pigeon.

Since you cannot hear
or maybe understand
what she is saying
I will translate.

She says
war is over
if YOU want it.

as in the market (Carmarthen), 1982

As in the market
a shot rang out—
it was the time of the siege of Lebanon—

as in the market
a shot rang out—
it was on my mind, it was on the news—

as in the market
a shot rang out—
the day of the worst was my son's 18th birthday—

as in the market
a shot rang out—
it was on my mind that he is grown—

as in the market
a shot rang out—
it was the time of the siege of Lebanon—

as in the market
a shot rang out—
it was on my mind, those could be my son—

as in the market
a shot rang out—
a slow day, time to think, it was on my mind,
it was the time of the siege of Lebanon,
it was on the news, they were someone's sons—

as in the market
a shot rang out,
there was quick silence, there was a buzz:

as in the market
a shot rang out—
(it was a joke) there was a buzz—

but it was on my mind,
it was on the news:
other markets, other mothers.

After trying to read Susan Griffin

What we have in common is not small
though sometimes seems so:
a cloud no bigger than a woman's hand,
the silver tilted moon:

What we have in common is not ours;
these winds, this storm,
the falling of sweet dreams and nearer leaves;
the harvest moon.

Diolch, Woody Guthrie

Sun yellow behind Port Talbot
orange in the rusted bracken,
far purple in the hills:
this land is your land,

this land is my land.

Advent poem for Jo

At Abergwen
the holly tree
is skirted
like bright dimity:

at Glangwili
the holly tree
is stately
in striped majesty:

in Llandysul
the holly tree
is pointed
like a Christmas tree:

but Abernawmor's
holly tree
beside the path
for all to see;

a funny shape
quite low and round,
thin branches ragged
to the ground

sings red and green
with treasure crowned:
the dearest tree
for miles around.

for Mrs Davies & Pencader Infants
Spring 1984

Early yellow daffodil
on the kitchen windowsill;

children with cold noses
see the first primroses;

frost all along the ridge,
snowdrops beside the bridge;

catkins swinging in the lane—
Spring's beginning here again.

time for bed

Watching a programme on foxes,
my daughter eats her supper:
flapjack, apple, milk.

The foxes live in Bristol
where they eat chicken
and chips, cardboard, rubbish.

Some people, mostly women,
feed the city foxes; bread,
a knuckle bone, some fat;

the foxes breed. Most
of the young are killed
before they reach one year

by civilisation; cars
or guns. Time for bed
I tell my well fed girl.

midsummer sevens

Little girls,
silly as jelly,
quick as fish
grubby as mud
or well thumbed walls
bright as periwinkles
straight as columbines:

your faces shine like buttercups,
new teeth white as may or daisies.

Little girls,
bubbly as suds,
new as lambs,
plump as smarties,
thin as whispers,
sharp as kittens,
cruel as a frost in June:

something grows in you, as hard
as the future, as near as hands:

something like song,
something like steel.

Variations on Cherryblossom, Mayday, 1984

Main Road, Tumble

In the shop window
a notice said 'cash only'
but in the shop garden
a cherry tree said spring.

King Street Carmarthen

Petal by petal,
Nott Square to St. Peter's
the cherry tree blossom
comes blowing to meet us,

till glory by glory
the trees of St Peter's,
still blesséd with blossom
are bowing to greet us.

Abernawmor, Pencader

Sweeping the kitchen floor—
crumbs, litter, grit, scraps
and plum blossom petals:

outside the kitchen door—
earth! sky! sun! wind!
everyone's favourite plum tree.

in memoriam

Blue, near purple: last year's hyacinths
                        growing back to bluebells:
blue, blue violet flower eggs, grape hyacinths
                        stolen from Glandŵr garden:
blue bellstar, scilla, bluebell's little sister:
bluebell: earth's sky, azure, lapis lazuli:
bluebell, path's dream, May's fragrance, June's sorrow:
blue bellflowers, harebells, near remembered blue:

but reach me a gentian, flower of imagination,
                        told by my brother:
reach me a gentian, flower of memory,
                        shared with my mother:
flower of Demeter, Blodeuwedd's forgotten mother:
reach me a gentian, that the circle may complete.

View from the bus-stop: war memorial

Head and shoulders
above the rooftops
the blind white soldier stands
at ease, left leg relaxed
and rifle rested:

the marble plinth below
tells all his golden names.

Head and shoulders
above the railings
a single schoolboy waits
at ease, right leg relaxed
and schoolbag ready.

This could be a photograph
and not a poem:
                    for

man and boy
and stone and flesh

in black and white
would tell it all

but their unknown and golden names,
and their shared view of Pencader.

changing forget-me-not

found in *Wild Flowers*
of Britain and Northern Europe

wood forgetmenot
field forgetmenot
water forgetmenot
changing forgetmenot
tufted forgetmenot
bur forgetmenot
creeping forgetmenot
pale forgetmenot
blue eyed Mary Madwort

found at the roadside
Waungader, Pencader

FORGETMENOTS'
BLUE FACES SAY
FORGETMENOT
FROM DAY TO DAY:
AND HOW COULD I
FORGET THE BLUE
EXCEPT FROM DAY
TO DAY I DO.

Sweet William and the Painted Lady

'The Painted Lady is a butterfly
of the nymphalid family, one
of the most spectacular
in our uncertain British climate.'
(*Readers' Digest Book of the Countryside*)

'Sweet Williams are old time
favourite flowers, biennial,
in new auricular-eyed and plain
self coloured varieties:'
(*The Gardeners' Enquire Within*)

but if you don't know sweet williams,
I can't tell you. Crimson, they are,
carmine, all the reds; magenta,
shocking, all the pinks; white,
striped, red and white: all the

reds, pinks; crimson, velvet, red.
Certainly they are made of velvet
and have something about them
of seaside rock and fruit drops:
red, clear green, bright pink and white.

Sweet sweet william, when I saw
a Painted Lady on your crimson—
well, sweet william, *wel* and well.

Viola tricolour

On a sunny day
in the month of May
I planted a packet of pansy seeds.

Imagined jewels of pansy flowers
(eager faces
in many places)

were overtaken by the weeds
o years ago
and failed to grow:

but first among the raspberries
and now beside the runner beans;
between the sage and rosemary,

little under the lemon tree,
stronger than thyme, random
and bright as blue borage,

they have flowered unhoped for,
unexpected, small, selfseeded
gifts of natural life,

'massed, open solitary flowers
with five unequal petals,
in bare or grassy places'—

wild pansies,
yellow, violet,
uncultivated graces.

Where the toadflax grows

I indexed my progress
through roses and hollyhocks,
southernwood, harebells,
primroses, bluebells.
I wrote about delphiniums,
remembered forget-me-nots,
and let who would consider
the lilies of the field.

I saw ground elder
ground under:
I recognised the ransoms
depleted by the roadworks,
and jack-by-the-hedge
sated with exhaust fumes:
for let who will remember
the lilies of the fields.

Now I know the verge
where the toadflax grows:
from the edge of the main road
I took Welsh poppy seeds:
I stole a piece of primrose root
and thus defied the E.E.C:
for let who can consider
the lilies and the fields.

Strip cartoon for radio

1. Moonwoman daydreams Earthman;
   his kindly alien body,
   his imagined listening.

2. Moonman announces he will conquer Earth.

3. Moonwoman makes sandwiches of moondust,
   to give Moonman a taste of his own.

4. Moonman leaves the moon. WHOOOSH!

5. Moonwoman prepares food and lessons,
   and tidies the dust into patterns.

6. The dust has settled. Moonwoman
   daydreams Earthman: his kindly
   alien body, his imagined listening.

7. LATER, she damps down the dust for the night,
   and goes to sleep, wondering if Moonman is okay.

8. Moonman eats his sandwiches and remembers home.

9. Moonman enters Earth's atmosphere through
   a hole in the ozone layer. WHOOSH!

10. Moonman travels the earth, researching.
    Sometimes he gazes at the moon. He is lonely,
    and wishes he had more sandwiches.

11. Moonman visits each of the quarters
    and corners of the world, ending with Europe.

12. Moonman realises Earth is already conquered,
but by whom? He decides to think about it.

13. Moonman meets a writer in a pub in west Wales.
They decide to collaborate on a book.

14. Moonman goes back to Earthman's place:
there is a full moon shining over the countryside.

15. They crack another bottle and discuss ideas.

16. Moonman gets into bed and falls asleep,
listening to the sounds of a country night,
and the murmur of conversation from another room.

NEXT WEEK . . .

What are Earthman and Earthwoman talking about?
How does Moonman cope with a polltax demand?
or Moonwoman with her growing sense of isolation?

bird and iron

1.

Poetry is a bird in the iron rafters
above Cardiff Central Market;
it lives by flying,
and lodges where it can.

It is the single sparrow, perched,
mute, head on one side,
asking for crumbs
when I have no bread.

It is the almost unheard
mindless chirrup, sweeter
than the kindly human din
of buying and selling.

Poetry knows nothing of money
or the daily grind of work,
though both are necessary
to the space it flies through.

Consider the crafted beauty
of the iron rafters. Poetry
made the space for me to think
of everyone who helped

to make a space for poetry.
Or I could put it like this:

bird and iron

2.

We know the name of Gwion
who stirred and sucked hot drops
of inspiration from his fingers:
but who made the cauldron?

We know the name of Ceridwen,
white Goddess of Caer Sidi,
spiral palace in the stars;
but who dug the siderite

hematite, bornite,
azurite, malachite,
calcite, barite,
fluorite, namuwite,

pyrite and chalcopyrite,
brookite and pyromorphite,
millerite, marcasite,
celestine, galena?

who dug the gypsum,
quartz and gold?
who dug the adit
and the shaft?

who crushed and smelted
the ore from the gangue,
the iron from the ore,
the gold from the dross?

which fathers and grandfathers,
mothers and grandmothers
worked like slaves
underground and overground

till Gwion became Taliesin
and Ceridwen Hen Wen?
Whose is the work
makes words, little bird?

bird and iron

3.

The diesel train
passes the steel works:
the iron horse
passes piebald ponies,

seagulls and sunshine,
Castell Nedd and Abertawe.
Dusk drops and rises
from Cardiff to Pencader.

Sparrows and seagulls,
ponies and people,
horses and humans
lodge where we can.

The stormy winds that shift

Magpie, black and white pied
pirate, unisex by uniform,
chatty as a machine gun
telling automatic terror;
blackthorn, barbed wire—bullies
often get their way.

The stormy winds that shift
the blackthorn and barbed wire,
bully's too small a word for them.
Brothers in war and lore, they're
gods demanding sacrifice, a tree,
an evening in, a human life.

Blackthorn's the best of the bunch
I suppose; bleak barrier,
bare in midwinter, gnarled
as arthritis; still in Spring
arching armoured blossom,
tiny fivefold white and single

flowers in spikes and billows.
Barbed wire's a different spike
or skiver, you can see its point
of view, even as it stands there
mute and thick. Cousin razor
wire's a bright and subtler

bully, standard lockout gear,
known to wink, but only
by accident. Do you a right
nasty accident, can razor
wire, if you can't see razor's
sharply shifting points of view.

It's a bullying society, let's
face it, always was. The
sacrifice to ancient gods of
danger, demons, death, was
a bull killed on wasteland,
keeping the god's disease away:

eyes and faces on all sides,
arms and feet on all sides,
a god no bigger than a thumb,
hidden in each labyrinthine
human heart, waiting for
sacrifice without consent:

youths and maidens lost
in the soul's wasteland.

October Frost, Llanllwni Mountain

This morning the mountains are luminous.
In those high depths, frost becomes mist, mist sky
invisibly. Silent earth steams gently
to leaden grey steel grey silver white clouds.
Thistledown and willowherb seed earthlight
into space, galaxies, the universe.

Once in the forest, unfrozen frost drips
from overhead beech and sycamore trees:
a southern thaw already, to rust red
orange brown green, the mountain's other side.

Fields steam fiercely behind high hedges,
as though in Iceland or New Zealand. Surely
the sun is nearer than Llandeilo,
and warmer than Golden Grove. Frost lingers
only in scraps, patches, pockets, and at
journey's end. Colours condense to violet,

blue cranesbill, leafless, frosted to a bell.

Earthjuice

An ancient hen, kindly imprisoned
against the fox or mink or marten
chatters her news or her intention:
the shorn sheep sleep or bleat or eat.

The human nestling upstairs wrestles
with double science, modular, while
psychedelics whirl the airwaves:
'I read the news today, o boy';

'love love love love love is all,
love is all you need.' Today's lesson,
though at least I thought so
half an hour ago, today's lesson

is that comfrey will rise again,
boasting magenta velvet buds,
drooping its dusky pinky flutes
in nines and elevens, dozens, tens;

salad burnet will rise again:
steadily onward upward outward,
the expanding universe brings us
salad burnet in fluffy crimson tufts:

feverfew will rise again, it is
already risen, and yellow Welsh
or orange poppies. Forget-me-nots
are not forgot, will rise again,

are risen. The sap is riz,
blessed earth juice, solution
of mineral salts, sugars, energy,
vigour, integrated science;

the sap is riz, will rise again,
but the sons of man and woman,
the daughters of woman and man
have but a few short days to live,

have not where to lay their head,
rise up like the grass and are cut down
and will not rise again, no sirree,
we will not see their like again,

the young women and the young men,
the babies and the children,
the beautiful, the maimed, the doomed
the blessed will not rise again.

They will not rise again who died
in war or peace, in love or hate,
by accident, heritance, indulgence,
starvation, they are gone for ever,

and will not rise again. Preachers
will not rise again, politicians,
priests have gone the way of flesh:
the king is dead dead dead amen,

and will not rise again, though
the foxglove rises tall and straight
with open mouth and mottled throat.
The skylark also rises,

broom meadowsweet and buttercup.
The columbine will rise again:
yea, though Wil denies their beauty,
and Myrddin cuts their bank, when

the long days come around, denied
or trashed, ignored or praised,
the gypsy columbine, more fair
than Solomon will flower; and

nettles will rise again foursquare
and flower and seed and droop:
and great and rosebay willowherb,
southernwood, lads' love, old man;

hittypitty, honeysuckle, wallflower,
rose, musk mallow, treemallow
peaseblossom rise between
sunwarmed greystone walls.

Gods and demigods may rise again,
patria, fauna, mores, Myrddin;
I have seen Myrddin shimmer
above the river below his hill.

Herons will rise again, up
from the bend in the Talog
flying north-east above Sarn Helen
to Pencarreg or the heronry:

foxgloves will rise and flower again,
oak and ash, holly and ivy, leaf
and flower. Gaia is returned,
Osiris, Adonis may rise again

reeds, wind and water, barley,
rose, anemone and pheasant's eye,
greygreen fennel; borage, blue,
its flowers like fresh fallen stars:

tansy and teasle will rise and rise
again, hogweed and foxglove, yellow
mullein and purple toadflax, lowly
plantain and yellow toadflax;

but old women who died on the road
or in their kitchen, old men
who died on the stairs
or in their beds all unawares,

the middle aged who died laughing
or wasting in pain, winning
or losing, forgetting or remembering,
they are lost to us for ever,

the young women and the young men
the babies and the children,
set alight or shot to pieces
born unlucky, wasted with disease,

believers, unbelievers, speechless
or don't knows, the damned, the maimed
the blessed, one off, unmatched,
unnoticed; unwashed or overwashed,

millionaire or refugee, singular,
imperfect, human, unique, each
looked their last on all things
and will not rise again, though

deathjets will rise again, have
risen, are flying even now
back to Menwith Hill or Bremen, flying
low over the Talog or the Tyweli,

following the rivers or the fields,
scaring children, wildlife, livestock,
raising adult thoughts of war
and death by fire from the sky.

Love is not all we need,
evil may overcome,
all we were saying was
give peace a chance.

Pestilence is back again,
diseases of starvation, diseases,
of pollution, cholera, diptheria,
hepatitis, AIDS, despair:

Love is not all we need,
love is not near enough,
all we were saying was
make love not war.

The lilies of Alltwalis Hill
are ransoms, reeking sweetly.
The lilies of Abergwili
are bluebells, and the lilies

in the gardens of Glangwili
and Carmarthen, white Easter
arum lilies rise again. Wake-
robin, little robin, ragged robin,

I have seen them all, herb robert,
jack-by-the-hedge, jack-go-to-bed,
sweet william, sweet cicely, sweet-
briar, bramble and field rose,

the gorse and the heather, blueberry
raspberry, blackberry, dewberry,
hawthorn, blackthorn, whitethorn,
gooseberry, strawberry, windflower

tufted hair and reed canary grass.
Soft floppy pink poppies, purple
heartsease, comfrey, borage, bugle
rise in spring to flower again

but not today. In the garden behind
me feverfew, meadowsweet, cranesbill
buttercup, willowherb, southernwood
yarrow and rose are dank and wet.

Today the sky is grey and rosehips
tremor in the wind. A tremor in the
earth: the world is shaken and forgets.
Today's lesson, at least I thought so

eighteen weeks ago. I read
the news, o boy. The answer my friend.
Today the rain is hard
and mud is silting up the yard.

Frost will sink the marigolds
and chill the mallow. When this
equinoctial rain is drained
and the ground firms up again,

soon, I'll move that sage bush,
from the raspberries, plant out
a rosemary, pot on the tarragon
and maybe split the marjoram.

Praise be

The art of conversation is not dead,
praise be, but goes on lively in farm kitchens
in Gwyddgrug where solid fuel stoves
called Rayburn or Aga burn day and night,
winter and summer, rubbish, wood and coal
bought in plastic sacks from the local shop
which has kept going, just, on petrol sales
from a single pump. Conversation goes
on there too, between the dog on the floor
and the dogfood on the shelf, the cheese
in the chiller and cheesecake in the tabloids.
Now I come to think of it conversation's
hardly dead at all, it's Internet
hype that made me think perhaps it was; that
and the difference between chatter, gossip,
and the elegant exchange across cultures,
genders and generations that was
my pleasure this morning at Pantrhodyn.

In Praise of Carnivores

Sudden the warm fox stink from the little thicket
between the great and lesser green and empty fields
and a surge of, a filling with something like love
but isn't love of course, like lust but lust for what,
not for any body, not for human beings;
love of mammals maybe, lust after carnivores,
quick brown warm red stinky mangy foxes, making
spring festival of love in open fields, taking
chance with inattentive adolescent rabbits,
crunching heads off optimistic chickens, living
by godly richly smelling earth wind and tree roots,
thickets, copses, hedges, coverts, woods and orchards.

Cat walks towards me on the bluebell footpath, black
and sweet, between blackthorn and bramble, briar and
beech, greeting me, the species barrier broken
by Rayburns and tinned meat, histories of sharing
the fire and the kill. She'll have a rabbit today
if she can. Silky black Lucky, this cat's brother,
killed a rabbit yesterday, and dragged it, half grown
and full dead to the woodshed, showing off to me.
He knew I'd be pleased and wanted the praise. Good boy
I said thinking of lettuces and brassicas.
Now I'm thinking of Mr MacGregor's garden
and Peter Rabbit panting in the potting shed.

I ate Peter Rabbit and the flopsie bunnies.
When I was seven mum bought them at the co-op
ready skinned and jointed. She made them into stew
with onions, simmering sometimes on the stove
for dinner on Wednesday or Saturday. I knew
nothing of Beatrix Potter, Cottontail, Peter,
Tom Kitten, anthropomorphism, Pigling Bland,
slaughterhouses or vegetarianism.
The stew or broth or *cawl* was warm and kindly made
with love and electricity, stainless steel pans
washed in a stone sink, drained and dried with a soft cloth.
Mr McGregor would have recognised the scene.

We have to be human or who would love the gorse
and the broom, the swifts and the swallows, the haltered
pony patient by the roadside, another black
cat leaping the hedgebank by the council houses,
robin, violets, columbine: even if love is
not the word, and even though words are not the thing.
Have to be complex, messily contradicting
myself from day to day or hour to hour, or how
can I love the fox, the rabbit and the sweet peas,
the cats, the squirrel and the runner beans, or how
can anyone knowing the truth about the world
and humans in it suffer the little children.

Late Snowdrops

I was pregnant when I first found snowdrops
here, under alder and hazel, and thinking
of my baby's naked garden, sheep
pasture and couch grass, bramble and barbed wire,
dug a clump of bulbs beside the river.

The garden and the baby grew and now
the snowdrops seem more naked than us all,
thin-stemmed wildlife in the leaf mould,
massed clumps of green stems with no flowers
yet, no white, no opening, no nodding.

Uncertain boundary between two farms,
the river has shifted as rivers do,
restless beyond guessing, the greatest work
under these alder and hazel trees
and today's blue sky and the small birds' song:

the river has shifted soil from tree roots
and some snowdrop clumps, leaving a stony
beach and promises small as a baby's
fingernail, of snowdrops, plain as new moons,
under the lambstail catkins and blue sky.

May: i) Carmarthen

The sun sets behind John Street
lighting St. Peter's carpark.
A common pink clematis
swagged along the garden walls
shows up an uncommon glow.

Lighter and higher apple
blossom lifts from its single
tree. Red may in the dark hedge
exchanges colour with the old
phone box and the red lines
of short term parking bays.

Day's
over. Everyone's off home.

May: ii) Gwyddgrug

This is the time
of silage and of columbine:

the whine of tractors
hidden from the eye;

a flat cut field
below a hedge of may,

stubbled to nothing
much in green and beige;

lark at the roadside
anxious for her eggs;

a calf escaped searches
the sweet way back;

scramble of lambs
scraping the earth stone bare;

and

nesting on the green
bank below the hedge

violet white or pink
gypsy or columbine

flowers, a parliament
of silent birds.

columbine: *aquilegia vulgaris*; *blodau'r sipsi* (gypsy flower): closely related to larkspur, *blodau'r hedydd* (larksflower).

Collecting the milk

A buzzard waits and watches for young rabbits.
The sound of a car braking on loose chippings
stirs him to lift half off today's chosen post,
between the track and Dolwen Fach's shaven field.
Buzzard rocks and then takes off, gliding over
green and yellow stubble from a silage cut.

In the chapel carpark, orange hawkweed lifts
above the half-trimmed verge. I thought it was lost.
Unexpectedly my mind matches hawkweed
with swallows: rare, fragile, sharing habitat.
I am in this poem. This is my square mile.
Squirrel cuts across my way and wagtails dip.

These are the friends of the earth, this is greenpeace.
Wil's pony draws her head back between barbed wire
strands as I pass, wondering what to write here.
It's urgent. Black plastic from last year's big bales
is partly problem and partly solution.
One o'clock pips. Kettle on, toaster on, news:

Hungarian paprika is luminous.

Nicotiana at New Road bus-stop, Llandysul

Something moonlike about tobacco
flowers, a plain flat pale face perhaps,
transparent wall in invisible air;
something they do to me stronger
than I was ready for at the bus stop.

Southernwood too, I was thinking
on the bus step, I know that scent,
strong as a leap in invisible air,
heart or whatever it is, soul
turning in joy to some returning,

some love perhaps or loves,
a garden plot, a border
of green tobacco flowers:
a clearing in the woods,
southernwood, wormwood,

and talk of love
strong as flowers
alive in invisible air,
plain as a known face,
lovely like the moon.

heedless

Midsummer days of blue sky and long sun
when this year's calves stray from their mother's side,
when the shorn sheep graze easy in the fields,
and this year's foal matches her mother's stride;

when bats as well as birds fly after dawn,
and rows of sticks stand proud for beans or peas,
when vegetables grow as fast as weeds
and frogs hide underneath great rhubarb leaves;

when villages have garden festivals,
and advertise their summer carnivals

are days made loud with military jets,
combustion and pollution in the raw.
The silage-feeder soars above the hedge
heedless, a tractor-driven dinosaur.

The bonds of the world

The element of physics is a moment:
larkspur blue against a greystone wall
and amethyst under the bluegrey sky;
ladybird on a daisy head, ladybird
at home on a grass blade in the sun.

Is it the bonds of the world are breaking?

Redder than leafbuds on a rosehedge stem
ladybirds woke early into false spring,
sunshine summoning them from leafmould, tree
bark and hedgeroots into a morning late
for snowdrops to open yet so early
for the slowly waking beetles it seemed
like an omen as I found them sunning
on the rosehedge stem, on an old oak leaf,
in the raspberry canes and under the tips
of last year's bramble leaves by the bonfire.

They hibernate in dozens says the book
and it turns out the lady in their name
is the same as St. Mary of the Snows
and sorrows, lady of consolation,
god in a female form, mother of all
who will allow a mystery at the heart
of the universe to have a human
name. Ladybirds are regarded with awe
everywhere in the world says the book, and
awe is what I recognise as feeling.

A redbrick terraced house with a view
over the River Wye to the Black Mountains,
a garden with rhubarb and montbretia
and a slab for feeding next door's chickens:

a yellowbrick terraced house with a view
from the back garden to the grey gasworks,
two crazy pathways meeting each other
and red and white roses rambling the walls:

the families disagreed on religion,
table manners, politics, cats and food,
but everyone allowed a ladybird
to land on their hand and hear them saying

ladybird ladybird fly away home.
I wonder if ladybirds understand
I thought, saying it softly as I sat
with the chickens on the slab in the sun.

After the ladybirds, red everywhere:
in single holly berries, uncovered
by the rake, in single hips and haws: red
in elder leafbuds and in alder flowers;
red lights in the holly tree's pale old bark,
Persephone's blush in Demeter's face.

Red from the earth's core, haematite, iron,
copper, carbon, atoms and molecules
transpired by radiating light and warmth
into living filaments, live creatures
stranded over land, red threads on female
hazel catkins, swaying in waves of wind.

Ladybird cold on a northfacing wall,
ladybird on the comfrey, ladybird
in leafmould, bared by bloodstained gardening gloves:
snow still on northfacing mountain slopes: red
in the dusky overhanging alder,
in bramble shoots and comrade robin's breast.

Is socialism red because blood's red
I wonder and is it the blood of living
or of death? This is my territory
said the robin. Keep digging. I like
berries and centipedes, not ladybirds;
I live on worms and spiders, not questions;

wisdom is under the roots of the tree.

The bonds of the world are broken open.
She's not my lady, He is not my god,
robin is not my comrade or teacher,
books are only words, I am not at home:
the tree of the knowledge of good and evil
has different roots from the tree of life.

This afternoon I found four ladybirds
under the heel of a raspberry cane
I was cutting and covered them with moss
and leaves. May they live on into summer
eating aphids in the sunshine, beetles

with forward pointing biting mouthparts; with
well developed compound eyes; with red front
wings and silky back ones; with six black spots;
related by name with the queen of heaven,
regarded with awe over the whole world,

ladybirds, begun to seem like gods.
Fly home ladybird from my garden cold
as stone, with a view to barren pasture,
bungalows and snowy hills, fly away,
sleep in leafmould under ash and blackthorn.

Not gods but tutors in mythology:
spring sunshine overtook the poem until
ladybirds were everywhere, on nettles
for soup and comfrey for compost, on sage
and marjoram for supper, on violas
for cheer and beauty, purple, yellow, cream:

lowly beetles slowly walking bare earth
out of the shade of my body towards
open sunlight; or resting, last year's red
on this year's green, heads pointing towards
the plants' green hearts, backs towards the warmest
sun we've had so far, beamed between leafless trees.

Ladybird ladybird this is your home,
the winter is over and summer is come.
Walk towards me over damp bare earth
from the periwinkle to the saxifrage,
from the shade I made into the sunshine:
the element of physics is a moment.

Bond the world ladybird, this is your home,
on the larkspur leaves by the greystone wall.
Bond the world, summer to summer, winter
to spring, mythology to holiness,
moment to moment, physics to knowledge,
people unknown with knowledge undeclared.

Council houses white above Llanfihangel
skyline: socialism bright in the sunshine:

two ladybirds on a bean pole at home
in the sun: having it off, cheering me up.

Driven fast along the motorway I
glimpsed a mist of blackthorn blossom half
hidden by the tree that sheltered it: like
a half remembered half imagined myth,
Persephone emerging radiant
from hell, Blodeuwedd skimming the branches

of the universe or of an ash tree,
mind's quotations revving heart's equations,
the car gaining the city, fantasy
holding my daughter silent behind me
turning the pages. This is the city,
this is the poem, heart's equation solved

and undeclared and untranslatable;
history to physics, mythology
to love, folklore to etymology,
atoms of earth to molecules of life,
garden to house and garden, red to green,
ladybirds to children and their parents,
stories to live by, vegetables to grow;
my lady's beetles to all humankind.

NOTES on 'The bonds of the world'.

1 *Is it the bonds of the world are breaking?* on page 66 is a quotation from Saul Bellow.

2 Demeter and Persephone are from Ancient Greek mythology. Demeter is queen of the fruitful earth and Persephone is her daughter. She symbolises the young corn and spring generally, spending the winter underground.

3 Blodeuwedd (Flower Face or Flower Queen) was conjured from oak, broom and meadowsweet flowers in a medieval Welsh story. Later in the same tale, she became an owl, forbidden to show her face in daylight, (p. 71).